Gin Tonica

Dedication *To Sara*

Senior Designer Barbara Zuñiga
Production Controller Mai-Ling Collyer
Editorial Director Julia Charles
Art Director Leslie Harrington
Publisher Cindy Richards
Drinks Stylist Lorna Brash
Prop Stylist Luis Peral
Indexer Hilary Bird

First published in 2017 by
Ryland Peters & Small
20–21 Jockey's Fields
London WC1R 4BW
and
341 E 116th Street
New York, 10029
www.rylandpeters.com

10 9 8 7 6 5 4

ISBN: 978-1-84975-853-6

A CIP record for this book is available from the
British Library. US Library of Congress CIP data
has been applied for.

Printed in China

Gin Tonica

40 recipes for Spanish-style gin & tonic cocktails

David T. Smith

photography by Alex Luck

RYLAND PETERS & SMALL
LONDON • NEW YORK

Contents

Introduction

The gin and tonic is, on the face of it, perhaps one of the simplest mixed drinks in the world. It has a long and illustrious history, which has taken place in many exotic and far-flung locations. It's not too much of a stretch that, in some ways, empires were built or at least maintained thanks to this drink. This simplicity does not mean that the drink is boring or that its preparation has been void of innovation; in particular, one variation – the Spanish Gin Tonica – has been at the forefront of both a revival in gin and a rise in the quality and craftsmanship of modern mixed drinks.

The earliest known reference to the 'Gin and Tonic' comes from an 1868 edition of *The Oriental Sporting Magazine* from India. The tonic that they refer to is an effervescent water flavoured with quinine and sweetened with sugar. At this time, quinine, an alkaloid which comes from cinchona bark, was a key medicine in the fight against malaria, a parasite spread by mosquitoes. Malaria plagued many of the Imperial outposts in India and Africa and eventually spread to the New World. In the late 19th century, the drink was cited in both medical and recreational contexts. In many places, alcohol was safer to drink than water and many of the botanical ingredients in gin were thought to have medicinal properties; for example, juniper was seen to be a digestive aid that also freshened the breath. Tonic water had the vital quinine, but the carbon dioxide which gave the drink its fizz was also seen to have been another aid to digestion. Finally, the citrus garnish (lime juice was prescribed to British sailors as a preventative measure against scurvy) gave the drinker some vitamin C.

So what is the Spanish Gin Tonica? It is a particular type of serve for a Gin and Tonic, using a large balloon-shaped glass, lots of ice, and a colourful and aromatic garnish. There are hazy anecdotes of the style going back to the late 1980s, but most contemporary accounts suggest that it started around 2008–09 in Northern Spain, in particular the Basque region. It arrived in the UK around 2011. Before the wide-scale availability of the Copa de Balón or 'Gin Tonica' glass, early versions of the drink were served in large Bordeaux wine glasses. Spanish ice is typically nearly twice the size of its British equivalent and so, when using a short glass, you can't fit much liquid in alongside the ice. Therefore in order to have enough ice to keep the drink cool, larger glasses were needed!

Creating a perfectly-paired Gin Tonica

Since 2005, the number of gins available across the world has increased from around 200 to over 2,500 in 2017. This increase has also inspired a boom in tonic water, in particular premium brands. After all, if drinkers are paying more attention to their choice of gin and will pay a little more for it, why not also invest in a better-quality tonic? Whereas consumers were once limited to Schweppes, supermarket own-brand, Britvic or Canada Dry, today there are more than 100 varieties to choose from, including tonics with flavours such as yuzu, mint, rosemary and even tomato. With such a wide variety of both gins and tonics on offer, it can help to know a little more about the flavour profiles of both The inclusion of new and imaginative garnishes came hand-in-hand with a rise in new gin distilleries, which were producing spirits with new and exciting botanicals and flavour profiles. For bars, elaborate garnishes in their Gin Tonica became a way to help them differentiate from competitors.

Gin flavour profiles usually fall within one, or a combination of two of the following categories:

Classic: a primary mix of piney juniper, earthy angelica and aromatic coriander. e.g. Gordon's, Tanqueray, Hayman's London Dry Gin.

Herbal: aromatic, leafy flavours such as basil, rosemary and bay leaves. e.g. Berkeley Square, St. George Terroir, The Duke Munich Dry Gin.

Floral: flavours of lavender, rose, camomile, and honeysuckle. e.g. Bloom, Golden Moon, Apothecary, Nolet's Silver.

Citrus: bright, vibrant flavours of citrus: lemon, lime, orange, grapefruit, lemongrass. e.g. Beefeater, Redsmith, Tarquin's, Hunter's, Bluecoat, Tanqueray No. Ten.

Sweet-Spicy: flavours of baking spice, nutmeg, cardamom, cinnamon, anise. e.g. Warner Edwards, Portobello Road, Big Gin, Hayman's Royal Dock, Plymouth Navy Strength.

Savoury/Peppery-Spicy: flavours of cumin and caraway, as well as the menthol pepper notes of black and pink peppercorns, grains of paradise, and cubeb berries. e.g. Bombay Sapphire East, Darnley's View Spiced, Opihr, Whittaker's Pink Peculier.

When it comes to tonic water, there are a few all-rounders that will mix well with almost any spirit; these include Fever-Tree Indian Tonic Water and Schweppes Indian Tonic Water (in the UK and Europe).

Some tonics have a signature character profile, such as the herbaceous Fever-Tree Mediterranean, the spicy Fever-Tree Aromatic and Fentiman's 19:05 Herbal Tonic Water. Some also have specific flavours, such as Original Yuzu Ocha, Fever-Tree Elderflower, Fentimans Pink Grapefruit and Double Dutch Cranberry.

Garnishes add visual flair and complement the aromas and flavours of the gin. Often, the first thing a drinker smells is actually the garnish and it is certainly the first thing to catch their eye. The go-to is a wedge of either lemon or lime, although other citrus fruits such as orange and pink grapefruit are becoming popular. Like gins, garnishes can be divided into different categories:

Herbs/Leaves: rosemary, basil, bay, coriander/cilantro, etc.

Spices: cinnamon sticks, star anise, peppercorns, etc.

Fruit: strawberries, blackberries, cranberries, melon, grapes, etc.

With so much choice, a drinker may be baffled by the possible options. When looking at combinations, there are two main schools of thought:

Option 1: match the flavours of the gin with the tonic and the garnish.

Option 2: choose flavours that contrast, but complement one another.

The truth, as is often the case, is usually in the middle. For example: Conker Spirit Gin includes elderflower as a botanical, and when combined with an elderflower tonic, this flavour really shines through. A garnish of elderflower or elderberries may be overkill, not to mention the possible seasonal impracticalities. Lemon is a good complement to elderflower and gives the drink a little zestiness. Tanqueray Gin is made without citrus, but has a clean, crisp flavour, so a wedge of lemon or lime (or both) adds a refreshing vibrancy.

A final word on garnishes: while it is important for a drink to look and taste good, keep in mind that it also needs to be practical to drink. Large garnishes that poke out of the glass might hit you in the face, and – at the other end of the spectrum – lots of 'bits' can make a Gin Tonica difficult to drink without a straw.

Ice & Glassware

Finally, two essential components for making a good Gin Tonica are ice and glassware. Ice is a key ingredient – it not only keeps the drink cool, but helps to fill the glass and create the visual spectacle associated with the drink. Ideally, cubes should not be smaller than 20 mm/¾ inch cubed (any smaller and it will melt faster and water down the drink). For the same reason, it is best not to use crushed ice. Store-bought ice is a good choice when making several drinks at once. It is cheap and quick and is usually crystal-clear; something that is difficult to replicate at home. Increasingly, shops are offering a variety of bagged ice: crushed; a larger bag of relatively small cubes, which are just about usable for Gin Tonica; and the Spanish-style, egg-sized cubes (cylinders or spheres), both of which are ideal. If using home-frozen ice, it is best to steer clear of novelty ice trays – the ice often melts quickly and can be difficult to remove from the tray. It is also worth investing in a sealed box that you can keep ice cubes in reserve. Once frozen, empty all the ice cubes into the box and refill the tray.

Gin Tonica tend to contain more gin (always a double measure), more tonic and more ice than most people's standard serves. As such, it requires a suitable glass. The Gin Tonica glass, aka Copa de Balón or Copa Glass, comes from Spain and looks like a large brandy balloon with a long stem. The stem is important, as it keep the drinker's hand away from the drink, keeping it colder for longer. The way that the glass narrows at the top helps to concentrate the aromas of the drink emanating from the gin's botanicals and the all-important garnish.

How to Make a Gin Tonica

1 Start off with a clean Gin Tonica glass.

2 Add fresh ice cubes to fill ¾ of the glass.

3 Stir gently for 15 seconds with a bar spoon or chopstick to chill the glass.

4 Pour away any liquid from the melted ice.

5 Top up the glass with more ice.

6 Add the gin, trying to ensure that you coat the ice as you pour.

7 Add the tonic water. Pouring slowly helps the tonic to keep its fizz.

8 Add your garnish.

9 Let rest for 30 seconds to allow the flavours to integrate with each other.

Classic

Here you'll find a selection of classic drinks embracing the spirit of the original sun-downer. All are dry, crisp and refreshing and make excellent thirst quenchers, whether before dinner, in the bar, or while keeping cool in exotic tropical climes.

The Evans

Some drinks are named after nothing more than their garnish, such as the Gibson Martini, which is garnished with a single pearl onion. The Evans Gin Tonica is another example that also answers the hotly debated question of Gin & Tonic drinks: do you garnish with lemon or lime? The answer with the Evans is both!

Tanqueray (the choice here) has been made since 1830 and is currently produced at Cameronbridge Distillery in Scotland. It has a simple botanical recipe: juniper, coriander seed, angelica root, and liquorice/licorice root. The two fresh citrus wedges add a lively zing to this drink.

50 ml/1¾ fl oz Tanqueray Export Strength London Dry Gin (43.1% ABV)

50 ml/1¾ fl oz Schweppes Indian Tonic Water

1 lemon wedge and 1 lime wedge, to garnish

Build the drink in the glass following the instructions given on page 9.

Other good choices of gin include Malawi Gin, Bedrock London Dry Gin and Filliers Dry Gin 28.

James Bond Gin Tonica

Although 007 is best known for his Vodka Martinis – shaken,
not stirred – he does enjoy other tipples from
time to time. In Ian Fleming's 1958 book, *Dr. No*,
James Bond makes a drink to this recipe when
he has just flown in to Jamaica.

Gordon's Gin (which Bond's recipe specifically calls for) comes
in a range of alcoholic strengths, from 37.5% ABV to 47.3%
ABV. Bond would have probably have used the 47.3% ABV
version, but the drink works well with the 37.5% ABV
version too.

50 ml/1¾ fl oz Gordon's Yellow Label Gin (47.3% ABV)

25 ml/1 fl oz lime juice (or juice of 1 lime)

lime shells from the squeezed lime, to garnish

150 ml/5 fl oz Schweppes Indian Tonic Water

Add the gin and juice to your glass. Add ice and shells
of the lime. Top-up with tonic.

Other good choices of gin include Tanqueray
and Tanqueray No. Ten.

Pink Gin Tonica

A drink long associated with the Royal Navy, the Pink Gin is a combination of gin and Angostura Bitters. For this recipe, the mix has been lengthened with tonic.

Plymouth Gin is a great choice; not just because of its strong Naval connections, but the gin has a bold and balanced flavour with the complexity of both spice and citrus.

In 2016, Fever-Tree released their pink Aromatic Tonic Water, blended with Angostura bark. This has a slightly different flavour to Angostura Bitters as, surprisingly, the latter does not actually contain any Angostura bark. The result is a herbaceous and spicy drink with a pleasant, cosy flavour.

50 ml/1¾ fl oz Plymouth Gin

150 ml/5 fl oz Fentimans Indian Tonic Water

5–6 dashes of Angostura Bitters

a lime wedge, to garnish

Build the drink in the glass following the instructions given on page 9.

Other good choices of gin include Hayman's Royal Dock Navy Strength, Ableforth's Bathtub Gin and Beefeater.

The Hartley

A Gin Tonica that borrows a key ingredient from another great gin drink: the Negroni.

This drink needs a solid, classic gin as its base in order to stand up to the bittersweet flavours of Campari. Loch Ness Gin, with its clean, bold character, is a great choice and the bright crispness of Franklin & Sons Indian Tonic completes the picture.

50 ml/1¾ fl oz Loch Ness Gin

150 ml/5 fl oz Franklin & Sons Indian Tonic Water

5 ml/1 teaspoon fresh orange juice

5 ml/1 teaspoon Campari

single slice of orange on a cocktail stick, to garnish

Add ice, gin and tonic to a Gin Tonica glass, then add the orange juice, followed by the Campari. Finally, add the garnish.

Other good choices of gin include Sipsmith, Tanqueray, Hayman's London Dry Gin, Puddingstone Campfire Gin and Conker Spirit Dorset Dry Gin.

Long Pedlar

Invented in the 1960s, bitter lemon is tonic water with added citrus. It was created as a mixer for vodka, but it also works well with gin, especially sloe gin.

Sloe gin is a sweetened liqueur gin that is flavoured with blackthorn (sloe) berries. Another name for these is 'pedlars' and there used to be a sloe gin brand of the same name based in Plymouth.

The Long Pedlar is a way of enjoying sloe gin in a long, refreshing drink. As sloe gin is traditionally drunk in the winter, this makes a good counterpart for summer.

The sweet, plump, jammy flavours of the sloe berries are balanced by the contrasting sharpness of the lemon tonic. It delivers a very complex flavour and is exceptionally refreshing.

50 ml/1¾ fl oz sloe gin (Hayman's or Plymouth)
150 ml/5 fl oz Fever-Tree Lemon Tonic
lemon peel and bay leaves, to garnish and, if in season, some sloe berries, ideally embedded in an ice cube

Build the drink in the glass following the instructions given on page 9.

For a drier drink, Whittaker's Gin of Harrogate have recently released 'Clearly Sloe' – a distilled, colourless sloe gin with all the jamminess, but none of the sweetness.

Gimlet Gin Tonica

The higher ABV of navy strength gin creates a greater concentration of botanical oils. This gives it a stronger flavour and means that it stands up to being paired with more robust mixers. This drink is inspired by the Gimlet – a traditional naval cocktail of gin and Rose's Lime Cordial (lime being an age-old preventative measure against sailors' scurvy).

The Isle of Wight Distillery have made a special navy edition gin in collaboration with HMS Victory, Admiral Nelson's flagship at Trafalgar. Another favourite, Royal Dock, refers to the dockyard at Deptford; Burrough's Distillery supplied Senior Service navy gin to ships there for many years.

50 ml/1¾ fl oz HMS Victory Navy Gin
100 ml/3½ fl oz East Imperial Old World Tonic
100 ml/3½ fl oz sparkling water/club soda
20 ml/⅔ fl oz Rose's Lime Cordial
lime wedges, to garnish

❋

50 ml/1¾ fl oz Hayman's Royal Dock Gin
150 ml/5 fl oz Schweppes Indian Tonic
5 ml/1 teaspoon lemon juice
5 ml/1 teaspoon lime juice
lemon and lime slices, to garnish

Build the drinks in the glass following the instructions given on page 9.

Yellow Gin Tonica

Gin is typically thought of as unaged, but, increasingly, distillers are experimenting with barrel-aged gin.

Hayman's Family Reserve

A lightly-aged spirit in the classic 'Yellow Gin' style that was popular in the 1950s and 1960s, this is reminiscent of the old Booth's House of Lords Gin.

50 ml/1¾ fl oz Hayman's Family Reserve

150 ml/5 fl oz Merchant Heart Indian Tonic Water

lime wedge, to garnish

Two Birds Sipping Gin

This aged gin is in a more modern style, and makes use of both European Oak and American Pecan woods. It is a powerful, nutty gin with an ochre glow.

50 ml/1¾ fl oz Two Birds Sipping Gin

125 ml/4 fl oz Fentimans 19:05 Tonic Water

fresh blackberries, to garnish

Build each drink in the glass following the instructions given on page 9.

Shortcross Gin Tonica

Shortcross Gin is made by the Rademon Estate Distillery in Northern Ireland using a combination of imported botanicals and those foraged from the estate itself. The gin is elegant and has a pleasant complexity with lots of fruit and spice notes. It is quite a sippable spirit, but also makes a great Gin Tonica.

The gin pairs well with Thomas Henry Tonic Water from Germany, which has a very clean and crisp flavour profile and allows the subtleties of the gin to shine through.

The orange garnish adds a sweet zesty flavour and aroma and the coffee beans provide a deep aroma that is exceptionally inviting.

50 ml/1¾ fl oz Shortcross Gin

150 ml/5 fl oz Thomas Henry Tonic Water

thin slice of orange, quartered, 3-4 coffee beans and a bay leaf, to garnish

Build the drink in the glass following the instructions given on page 9.

Other good choices of gin include Crossbill and Shetland Reel.

Contemporary

These recipes represent a 21st-century take on the Gin Tonica. With more unusual and exotic flavours, gins sourced from around the world, and an adventurous approach to garnishes.

Sublime Gin Tonica

This drink is inspired by the Sublime Moment Martini invented by Sam Carter and served at the Bombay Sapphire Distillery at Laverstoke Mill. The pairing of the garnishes generates a phenomenon called transmogrification, whereby two flavours – here, vanilla and pink grapefruit – combine to create a third, unrelated flavour – in this instance, chocolate.

The gin is soft and elegant and the tonic is clean, which means that the full impact of the garnish can be appreciated. Because a lot of the flavour of the drink is derived from the garnish, this drink makes a good non-alcoholic choice (minus the gin, of course).

50 ml/1¾ fl oz Bombay Sapphire

150 ml/5 fl oz Fever-Tree Indian Tonic Water

vanilla pod/bean slivers and a pink grapefruit wedge, to garnish

Build the drink in the glass following the instructions given on page 9.

Other good choices of gin include Blackwater No.5 and Silent Pool.

The Earl

Tea is a great accompaniment to gin and it is quick and easy to infuse. There are a huge range of suitable tea bags available. Companies such as Infugintonic make infusion bags that are specifically paired with certain gins, but your average supermarket has a great range of suitable teas such as lemon & ginger, or raspberry & echinacea. Another great choice is Earl Grey, which has rich aromas and a zesty flair from the bergamot.

50 ml/1¾ fl oz East London Liquor Co. Premium Gin Batch No. 1

1 Earl Grey tea bag

150 ml/5 fl oz Schweppes Tonic Water

long piece of orange peel, to garnish

Add the gin to a glass and add the tea bag; allow to infuse for 60 seconds before using the mixture in your Gin Tonica. Then build the drink in the glass following the instructions given on page 9.

Other good choices of gin include Tanqueray and Beefeater.

Smoky Gin Tonica

Another tea that works well with gin is the smoky and intense Lapsang Souchong, which is a black tea that has been smoke-dried over pinewood fires. The slightly resinous quality from the pine is a great complement to a similar flavour that comes from juniper berries.

Hayman's London Dry Gin is a classic and robust gin with enough strength of flavour to mix well with this smoky tea.

50 ml/1¾ fl oz Hayman's London Dry Gin

1 Lapsang Souchong tea bag

150 ml/5 fl oz Original Classic Tonic Water

fresh lemon peel, to garnish

Add the gin to a glass and add the tea bag; allow to infuse for 60 seconds before using the gin in your Gin Tonica. Then build the drink in the glass following the instructions given on page 9.

Other good choices of gin include East London Liquor Co. Premium Gin Batch No. 2.

OB1

This Gin Tonica is made using a brand new gin from The Kyoto Distillery in Japan, which uses rice alcohol as a base spirit. Its botanicals include bamboo leaves, green tea and yuzu. The drink's name was inspired the designation code of the gin's initial Japanese release, OB1...

The gin is paired with a yuzu-flavoured tonic water from Original. Rather than a yuzu overload, the result is a bright and zesty drink that truly captures the complex floral and oily citrus character of the fruit. (Yuzu is a citrus fruit from East Asia that is popular in Japanese cuisine. It has both the tartness of the lime and the sweet, floral notes of lemon.)

50 ml/1¾ fl oz Ki No Bi Gin

150 ml/5 fl oz Original Yuzu Ocha Tonic Water

yuzu peel and leaf, to garnish, (alternatively a small piece of lemon and lime peel)

Build the drink in the glass following the instructions given on page 9, but use 1–2 Spanish-style ice spheres instead of regular ice cubes.

Other good choices of gin include Jinzu and Tanqueray No. Ten.

The Moon
Under Water

Named after George Orwell's 1946 essay on his view
of the perfect pub, this drink uses spirits from the Golden
Moon Distillery in the city of Golden, Colorado.

Golden Moon Gin brings fruity, earthy and floral flavours
as well as some dry juniper and lemon. The Crème de Violette
is made using violet flowers and adds a little sweetness
and floral complexity to the drink, with the garnish adding
some visual flair.

50 ml/1¾ fl oz Golden Moon Gin

100 ml/5 fl oz Schweppes Tonic Water

5 ml/1 teaspoon Crème de Violette

small lime wedge and 2-3 edible flowers, to garnish

Add the gin and ice to your glass, then add the tonic water.
Slowly pour the Crème de Violette over the top of the drink,
before adding your garnish.

French Vineyard

G'Vine is a French gin made with grape alcohol and botanicals that include grape vine flowers. Peter Spanton No: 1 London Tonic is a relatively clean and classic mixer, which allows the aromatics of the gin to come through.

The frozen grapes add an extra chill factor without watering down the drink, and – after a few minutes– this garnish is soft enough to eat.

50 ml/1¾ fl oz G'Vine Floraison Gin

120 ml/4 fl oz Peter Spanton No. 1 London Tonic

3 frozen white grapes and 3 frozen red grapes,
to garnish

dash of Orange Bitters

Build the drink in the glass following the instructions given on page 9.

Other good choices of gin include Chilgrove Dry Gin.

Big Ben

This is a variation on a more established drink: Bénédictine and tonic water. Bénédictine is a botanical liqueur flavoured with various herbs and spices, which is made in Fécamp in Normandy, France.

Big Gin, made by Captive Spirits near Seattle in the state of Washington, USA, has a rich and balanced flavour with bright spice and a lingering warmth from Tasmanian pepperberry (also known as Cornish pepper leaf).

The orange works well with the spice flavours and just takes the edge off of the drink's sweetness. The result is a complex and warming Gin Tonica that is nonetheless very refreshing.

50 ml/1⅔ fl oz Captive Spirits Big Gin

100 ml/3½ fl oz Thomas Henry Tonic Water

50 ml/1⅔ fl oz Soda Water

25 ml/1 fl oz Bénédictine Liqueur

a sprinkling of crushed pink peppercorns, to garnish

orange wedge or a long ribbon of orange peel (optional)

Build the drink in the glass following the instructions given on page 9.

Caledonian

Scotland has long been associated with whisky production, but it has recently experienced a boom in the opening of small gin distilleries across the country. The Glasgow Distillery Co. makes a bold, juniper-forward gin called 'Makar Gin'. It partners well with Walter Gregor – a tonic water made in Aberdeenshire, Scotland.

This drink combines these ingredients to make a bold and flavoursome Gin Tonica with a twist. The choice of whisky makes a difference to the drink: a blend or Highland adds a woody mellowness, whilst a splash of Islay can bring an intense and aromatic smokiness.

50 ml/1¾ fl oz Makar Gin

200 ml/6¾ fl oz Walter Gregor Tonic Water

10 ml/2 teaspoons Scotch Whisky – Johnnie Walker Red or Highland Park 12, for example.

long piece of orange peel and a pinch of nutmeg, to garnish

Build the drink in the glass following the instructions given on page 9.

Other good choices of gin include Crossbill, and for an extra special drink, Crossbill 200.

Experimental

An innovative selection of drinks that
really push the frontier of Gin Tonica
and – occasionally – turn the concept
on its head. These quirky and colourful
drinks are sure to impress your guests.

Gin Tonica Float

The ice-cream float is a childhood favourite and tastes as good today as it did back then. This gin and tonic variant uses lemon sorbet for a more tart flavour, but has a similar effect to the ice-cream in a float. The point of perfection with this drink is when the sorbet starts to melt and you suck little bits of it up through the straw. It is indulgent, but a lighter alternative to a pudding, or a way to liven up your sorbet.

The drink has great potential for experimentation using different gins and sorbet flavours. Blood orange sorbet adds an extra zing, whilst blackcurrant would add more tartness. You could even use Champagne sorbet for a more regal quality.

50 ml/1¾ fl oz Beefeater Gin

150 ml/5 fl oz London Essence Co. Classic London Tonic Water

1 large scoop of lemon sorbet

finely cut lemon peel strips, to garnish

Combine the gin and tonic in the glass and then add a scoop of sorbet, being sure that it doesn't fizz up and cause your glass to overflow.

Other good choices of gin include Bluecoat American Dry Gin, Redsmith London Dry Gin and Hunters Cheshire Gin.

Spanish Strawberry

In 2015, a new phenomenon arrived in Spain: strawberry gin. Such was the popularity of this product in its birthplace of Valencia that within months, another six had entered the market and, by the end of 2016, there are over 30 strawberry-flavoured gins.

In Valencia, the Strawberry Gin Tonica is not actually made by pairing the gin with tonic water, but rather Lemon Fanta, a slightly tart soft drink. The result is a slightly cloudy drink with a pinkish hue; the garnishes add visual brightness. The Lemon Fanta makes the drink sweeter than a normal Gin Tonica, so the use of Blackwater Strawberry Gin (one of the drier ones on the market) gives the drink balance. For a tarter drink, try substituting the Lemon Fanta for Bitter Lemon.

50 ml/1¾ fl oz Blackwater Strawberry Gin

120 ml/4 fl oz Lemon Fanta

fresh or frozen strawberries, quartered,
and curled lemon peel, to garnish

Build the drink in the glass following the instructions given on page 9.

Another good choice of gin is Poetic License Strawberries and Cream Picnic Gin.

Goldfish Bowl

This drink is inspired by the nickname of the copita glass: 'goldfish bowl'. It is made using a bright and zesty gin from Sweden, paired with a combination of lemon tonic and lemonade, plus a splash of Blue Curaçao.

The garnish is rather unusual, but partly inspired by the practice in some bars in Spain of serving a gin tonic with gummy sweets. The fish shapes complete the aquarium look.

50 ml/1¾ fl oz Hernö Gin

10 ml/2 teaspoons Blue Curaçao

150 ml/5 fl oz Schweppes Bitter Lemon

50 ml/1¾ fl oz lemonade or lemon & lime soda

fish-shaped gummy sweets and rosemary sprigs,
to garnish

Build the drink in the glass following the instructions given on page 9.

Rocktail

A trip to the British seaside is not complete without a stick of rock as a memento. This drink embraces Brighton's history as a seaside resort with its eponymous gin.

Brighton Gin is soft and light, and a pleasure to sip on its own. The inclusion of a small piece of rock is a visual delight and, over time, the fresh, minty flavour transfers into the drink itself, making this a fun, flavour-changing Gin Tonica.

50 ml/1¾ fl oz Brighton Gin
120 ml/4 fl oz Fever-Tree Indian Tonic Water
little sticks of rock candy, to garnish

Build the drink in the glass following the instructions given on page 9.

Reverse Gin Tonica

Quinine is a key ingredient in a gin tonica and it usually comes from the tonic water, but what if it was distilled as one of the gin's botanicals? This is exactly what some producers have done, including 1897 Quinine Gin from Atom Supplies. Their theory is that by simply adding sparkling water/club soda, you will be able to create a dry gin and tonic.

As the drink contains no tonic water, it also has no sugar or sweetener and results in a clean, dry and crisp drink; as such, it requires a simple garnish: a thin piece of lemon or lime peel does a great job. If available, a thin slice of blood orange is even better.

50 ml/1¾ fl oz 1897 Quinine Gin

200 ml/6¾ fl oz sparkling water/club soda

thin slice of lemon and lime threaded through a cocktail stick, and two bay leaves, to garnish

Build the drink in the glass following the instructions given on page 9.

Another good choice of gin is Distillerie de Paris's Tonik Gin.

Sharish Gin Tonica

One of the most recent innovations in gin is the inclusion of an infused ingredient, such as blue pea flowers, in the gin. This makes the gin a light blue-purple colour until it is mixed with an acidic liquid such as lime juice or tonic water.

Sharish Blue Magic Gin from Portugal is one such example. This light violet gin changes to a light rose shade when tonic is added. The result is a floral and fruity drink, the flavours of which are neatly balanced when combined with the gentle zest of an orange wedge garnish. For those who desire a tarter drink, a grapefruit wedge is suggested.

50 ml/1¾ fl oz Sharish Blue Magic Gin

200 ml/6¾ fl oz Indi & Co Indian Tonic Water

orange or grapefruit wedges, threaded onto
a large cocktail stick

Build the drink in the glass following the instructions given on page 9.

Another good choice of gin is Ink Dry Gin
from Husk Distillers, Australia.

Cloudy Gin Tonica

In modern gins, the essential oils from botanicals can sometimes make a gin turn slightly milky or cloudy when water or tonic are added. This is known as 'louching', which is common in the drinking of absinthe. It does not mean that the gin is faulty, just that it has more botanical oil and, hence, is more likely to have a stronger botanical flavour. Here are two 'cloudy' recipes to try.

50 ml/1¾ fl oz Whittaker's Pink Peculier Gin

200 ml/6¾ fl oz Fever-Tree Indian Tonic

pink peppercorns and lime peel, to garnish

✳

50 ml/1¾ fl oz Cotswolds Gin

150 ml/5 fl oz Fentimans Naturally Light Tonic

bay leaves, to garnish

Build the drinks in the glass following the instructions given on page 9.

Late Breakfast

Probably more of a brunch than a breakfast drink, this utilises FEW Breakfast Gin from Illinois, USA. Along with some classic gin botanicals, their botanical mix includes bergamot and Earl Grey. Sticking with the breakfast theme, the drink also uses a dollop of marmalade.

The higher ratio of mixer to spirit makes this a lighter drink, perfect for when you still have at least half the day still ahead of you.

50 ml/1¾ fl oz FEW Breakfast Gin

150 ml/5 fl oz Fever-Tree Indian Tonic Water

150 ml/ 5 fl oz sparkling water/club soda

1 heaped teaspoon of marmalade, to garnish

dried orange slice, to garnish

Build the drink in the glass following the instructions given on page 9.

Another good choice of gin is Mason's Yorkshire Tea Gin.

Companion Tonic

A few gins have taken their quest for the perfect tonic water one step further by creating a bespoke tonic that perfectly complements their gin.

Le Tribute Gin

A more recent addition to the companion tonic world is Le Tribute from Spain; it has a citrus-led botanical mix, including lemon, lime, kumquat, tangerine, orange and lemongrass. Fresh basil leaves add a herby freshness.

50 ml/1¾ fl oz Le Tribute Gin

200 ml/6¾ fl oz Le Tribute Tonic Water

fresh basil leaves, to garnish

6 O'Clock Gin

6 O'Clock Gin & Tonic, made by Bramley & Gage, was one of the first of this kind of companion gins and tonics, and has light flavours of citrus and elderflower.

50 ml/1¾ fl oz 6 O'Clock Gin

200 ml/6¾ fl oz 6 O'Clock Indian Tonic Water

pink grapefruit wedge, to garnish

Build each drink in the glass following the instructions given on page 9.

Gum & Tonic

Gum (Gin + Rum) is unusual in that it contains two different spirits; the rum adds base character to the botanical flavours of the gin. Using white or unaged rum results in a lighter drink, whilst an aged rum will add more deep, complex wood and spice notes. I've given recipes for both styles here.

Light Gum & Tonic

30 ml/1 fl oz Whittaker's Gin

20 ml/⅔ fl oz white rum (Botran Reserva Blanca or Havana Club Anejo 3 Años)

200 ml/6¾ fl oz Fever-tree Indian Tonic Water

pineapple flags and lime peel, to garnish

Dark Gum & Tonic

30 ml/1 fl oz Sipsmith Gin

20 ml/⅔ fl oz Wood's, Pusser's or Lamb's dark rum

200 ml/6¾ fl oz Franklin & Sons Natural Light Tonic Water

Build each drink in the glass following the instructions given on page 9.

Seasonal

The Gin Tonica is something that can
be enjoyed year-round and allows
drinkers to take advantage of seasonal
fruits and fragrant spices for its
garnish. Here are a series of recipes
to inspire you to enjoy the drink,
no matter the season.

Autumnal Gin Tonica

Darnley's View Spiced has a fine array of sweet and savoury spiced notes that are comforting as the nights start to draw in. Paired with Double Dutch's Cranberry Tonic, the result is a crisp, yet cosy drink. Garnish with in-season fruit such as cranberries and, for an extra zing, a thin piece of fresh ginger root.

50 ml/1¾ fl oz Darnley's View Spiced Gin

150 ml/5 fl oz Double Dutch Cranberry Tonic Water

fresh cranberries, thin slivers of fresh ginger root and rosemary sprigs, to garnish

Build the drink in the glass following the instructions given on page 9.

Another good choice of gin is Opihr Oriental Spiced Gin.

Winter Gin Tonica

Gin Tonica is not normally associated with the colder winter months, but that doesn't mean that there aren't great drinks to enjoy. This example uses Warner Edwards Gin, which has pleasant, warm, spiced notes and in addition to tonic, there is ginger ale in the mix, too.

50 ml/1¾ fl oz Warner Edwards Gin

75 ml/2½ fl oz Schweppes Tonic Water

75 ml/2½ fl oz Schweppes Ginger Ale

5 ml/1 teaspoon ginger wine or
The King's Ginger Liqueur (optional)

orange wedge studded with 3-4 cloves,
extra cloves and a cinnamon stick.

Build the drink in the glass following the instructions given on page 9.

Other good choices of gin include Portobello Road Gin and Edinburgh Gin.

Summer Gin Tonica

Summer is the key season in the Gin Tonica calendar and, with fine, warmer weather, there are plenty of opportunities to enjoy the great outdoors with a delicious drink.

Redsmith Gin is a recent release from the Nottingham-based distillery of the same name. It has bright citrusy and coriander notes and pairs well with the complex zestiness of The London Essence Co.'s Grapefruit & Rosemary Tonic Water.

The trio of citrus garnishes suggested here adds colour and allows the drinker to add a little more sourness if they desire.

50 ml/1¾ fl oz Redsmith Gin

150 ml/5 fl oz The London Essence Co. Grapefruit & Rosemary Tonic Water

wedges of lime, lemon and orange, to garnish

Build the drink in the glass following the instructions given on page 9.

Other good choices of gin include Beefeater, Hunters Cheshire Gin, Bluecoat and Tanqueray No. Ten. Another good tonic water is Fentimans Indian Tonic Water.

Spring Gin Tonica

Spring is a lively time of year, full of new life and some great seasonal produce. Conker Gin is made in Dorset on the South coast of England and is crafted using botanicals including rock samphire and elderflower. When paired with an elderflower tonic such as that from Fever-Tree, this botanical is highlighted and comes through a lot more. For extra complexity, London Essence Co.'s Orange and Elderflower Tonic is another good alternative.

50 ml/1¾ fl oz Conker Spirit Dorset Dry Gin

150 ml/5 fl oz Fever-Tree Elderflower Tonic

rhubarb stalk strips, lemon peel and lemon slice, to garnish

Build the drink in the glass following the instructions given on page 9.

Other good choices of gin include Knockeen Hills Elderflower Gin and Darnley's View Gin.

Chocolate Gin Tonica

Chocolate is a popular flavour with many people, but when it is used in drinks it is typically associated with rich creamy, dessert-like cocktails rather than the gin tonica.

This drink uses McQueen Mocha Gin, which is 100% distilled and features cocoa nibs, coffee and vanilla as part of its botanical mix. Whilst the chocolate-coffee flavours of mocha are obvious, the dryer, more traditional flavours of juniper and angelica are evident as well.

The choice of Cardamom Tonic adds a little sweetness and some aromatic spice, as well as a touch of ginger. The dark (bittersweet) chocolate notes of the bitters finish the drink off nicely, bringing the flavours together, adding depth and creating the perfect gin tonica for Valentine's Day.

50 ml/1¾ fl oz McQueen Mocha Gin

200 ml/6¾ fl oz Peter Spanton No. 9 Cardamom Tonic Water

3–4 dashes of Hotel Chocolat Cocoa Bitters

chocolate or sugar syrup, chocolate flakes and chopped pistachios, to garnish (optional)

First prepare the glass by dipping the rim in chocolate or sugar syrup and then into a saucer of chocolate flakes. Build the drink in the glass following the instructions given on page 9.

Another good choice of gin is X-Gin from Belgium.

Halloween Gin Tonica

One of the little known characteristics of tonic water is that it glows under ultraviolet light, so it makes quite an alluring drink in the right setting.

The gin of choice for this recipe is Maidstone Gin from Maiden Distillery. Maidstone has a long history of distilling and, at one point, the Bishop's Distillery in the town produced 3,000 gallons (3,600 US gallons) of Maidstone Hollands Gin each week.

Maiden Gin has a light sweetness and complex, spiced character that is complemented by the zestiness of Fentimans Tonic Water. The watermelon balls with juniper berries used as a garnish in this gin tonic add a succulent fruitiness and give the spooky illusion of eyeballs floating in your drink.

50 ml/1¾ fl oz Maidstone Gin

125 ml/4¼ fl oz Fentimans Indian Tonic Water

watermelon 'eyeballs', to garnish

The watermelon 'eyes' are made by using a melon baller to extract the watermelon balls and then placing juniper berries for the pupils.

Build the drink in the glass following the instructions given on page 9.

Christmas Gin Tonica

An alternative to Bucks Fizz or Champagne, this drink uses Sacred Christmas Pudding Gin, which is made by distilling gin that has been infused with Christmas puddings. These particular Christmas puddings have been handmade by Sacred distiller, Ian Hart. The tonic really brings out the rich spices and deep, fruity notes of the gin.

For those in Australia, Four Pillars have also recently released a Christmas Pudding Gin.

50 ml/1¾ fl oz Sacred Christmas Pudding Gin

150 ml/5 fl oz Schweppes Indian Tonic Water

selection of dried fruit (cranberries, apricot, raisins), to garnish

Build the drink in the glass following the instructions given on page 9.

Alternative recipe
(ideal for Christmas Day morning)

20 ml/⅔ fl oz Sacred Christmas Pudding Gin

75 ml/2½ fl oz Schweppes Indian Tonic Water

orange peel, to garnish

Serve in a Champagne flute with a thin piece of orange peel.

New Year's Gin Tonica

The end of the year deserves a special celebratory gin tonic. This bright and crisp drink is a great way to say goodbye to one year and welcome in the next.

The drink uses Hammer & Son Old English Gin, which is lightly sweetened and has a full, spicy character. Even the bottle has a festive air, as the gin is packaged in old Champagne bottles. Fever-Tree Tonic Water has a pleasant crispness and the Brut Champagne adds both extra fizz and a little dryness.

50 ml/1¾ fl oz Hammer & Son Old English Gin
200 ml/6¾ fl oz Fever-Tree Indian Tonic Water
50 ml/1¾ fl oz Brut Champagne
(or other dry sparkling wine)
3 dashes of Orange Bitters
flamed orange peel, to garnish

Build the drink in the glass following the instructions given on page 9.

Credits

The author and the publishers would like to thank all the distilleries and tonic producers who so generously supplied their wonderful gins and tonics used in both the recipe testing and photography for this book.

1897 Quinine Gin
www.masterofmalt.com/gin/
1897-quinine-gin/

Beefeater Distillery
www.beefeatergin.com

Big Gin
www.captivespiritsdistilling.com

Blackwater Distillery
www.blackwaterdistillery.ie

Bombay Sapphire
www.bombaysapphire.com

Brighton Gin
www.brightongin.com

Conker Gin
www.conkerspirit.co.uk

Cotswolds Distillery
www.cotswoldsdistillery.com

East London Liquor Company
www.eastlondonliquorcompany.com

FEW Spirits
www.fewspirits.com

Golden Moon Distillery
www.goldenmoondistillery.com

G'Vine
www.g-vine.com

Hammer & Sons
www.oldenglishgin.com

Haymans Gin
www.oldtomgin.co.uk

Hernö Distillery
www.hernogin.com

Isle of Wight Distillery
www.isleofwightdistillery.com

Jensen's Gin
www.bermondseygin.com

Ki No Bi Gin
www.kyotodistillery.jp

Le Tribute
www.letribute.com

Loch Ness Gin
www.lochnessgin.co.uk

Makar Gin
www.glasgowdistillery.com/makar-gin

Martin Miller's Gin
www.martinmillersgin.com

McQueen Gin
www.mcqueengin.co.uk

Plymouth Gin
www.plymouthgin.com

Redsmith Distillery
www.redsmithdistillery.com

Sacred Spirits Company
www.sacredspiritscompany.com

Sharish Gin
www.sharishgin.com

Shortcross Gin
www.shortcrossgin.com

Sipsmith
www.sipsmith.com

Southwestern Distillery
www.southwesterndistillery.com

St. George Spirits
www.stgeorgespirits.com

Union Distillers
www.twobirdsspirits.co.uk

Warner Edwards
www.warneredwards.com

Whittaker's Gin
www.whittakersgin.com

Bénédictine
www.benedictinedom.com

1724 Tonic
www.1724tonic.com

Double Dutch Drinks
www.doubledutchdrinks.com

East Imperial Tonic
www.eastimperial.com

Fentimans
www.fentimans.com

Fever-Tree
www.fever-tree.com

Franklin & Sons
www.franklinandsons.co.uk

Indi & Co Tonic
www.indidrinks.com/en/

London Essence Company
www.londonessenceco.com

Merchant Heart
www.merchantsheart.co.uk

Q Tonic
www.qtonic.com

Schweppes
www.schweppes.com

Thomas Henry Tonic Water
www.thomas-henry.com

Walter Gregor's Tonic Water
www.summerhousedrinks.com

Author's Acknowledgments

In addition to the gin distilleries and tonic companies whose products were used in the recipes, I would like to thank the following people for their help with this book: The Gin Archive, Nicholas Cook of The Gin Guild, Aaron J Knoll, Clayton & Ali Hartley, Joe Barber, Roberto of Cappuccino Bar in Spain, Bernadette Pamplin, Cherry Constable, Dr. Anne Brock, Gin Miller, Julia Nourney, Robert Evans, IL Fleming, Ian Hart, Hilary Whitney, Olivier Ward, Emma Stokes, Alberto Pizarro, Sarah Mitchell, Adam Smithson, Sam Carter, Stephen Gould, Helen Chesshire, Jon Hillgren, The Hayman Family, Henrik Hammer, Craig Harper, Dan Szor, Eric Zandona, Bill Owens, Natasha Bahrami, Hannah Lanfear, Michael Vachon, David W Smith, JP Smith, Holly Robinson and Ben Capdevielle. I'd also like to thank my publisher Julia Charles, along with Leslie Harrington, Barbara Zuñiga and the rest of the team at RPS who have been a treat to work with, and thanks also go to Alex Luck, Lorna Brash and Luis Peral for creating the beautiful photographs. Finally a special thanks to Sara Smith, without whom the book would not be possible.

Index